"*Plucking the Strings* is
who want to celebrate
delightful, creative, pra
healing. I especially appreciated the feminine imaging of God, the 'contemporary' appeal, and musical tone of her psalms. What a rich treasury of poetic prayer for the poet within all of us!"

Bridget Mary Meehan, Author
God Delights in You; Exploring the Feminine Face of God; and
Affirmations from the Heart

"This is truly a delightful book! The psalm-poems are not only most accessible, but also full of depth and inspiration. As a personal, do-it-yourself psalm book, it can fit beautifully into a busy work day as well as a retreat and is sure to enrich anyone who follows its simple but creative program."

Thomas G. Hand, S.J.
Retreat Director and Meditation Teacher,
Mercy Center, Burlingame, CA

"In this personal journal, Joan Metzner provides us with an opportunity to be psalmists: to pray our love, our rage, our compassion, our concern, our hopes, and our fears. In short, Joan helps us pluck the prayer strings of our hearts."

Sandra DeGidio, O.S.M.
Author, *Sacraments Alive* and
Prayer Services for the Elderly

"Joan Metzner's *Plucking the Strings* reflects something that one finds in Thomas Aquinas and John Calvin, as well as in the Book of Psalms: the truth that all creation bears 'vestiges' or 'traces' of the Trinity (as Aquinas has it); the 'marks' or 'sparks' of the Creator (as Calvin renders it). This book is image-rich and experience-based and relies on what we encounter every day all around us to provide the impulse for prayer."

Sister Pamela Smith, SS.C.M.
Director, Lay Ministry Programs,
SS. Cyril and Methodius Seminary
Orchard Lake, MI

"This book is not only inspiring, but also creative, as it gently suggests to readers that they can be psalmists of their personal spiritual journeys. It definitely comes from the heart and witnesses to 'walking in the Spirit.'"

Dr. Marcella Hoesl, M.M.
Oblate School of Theology
San Antonio, TX

"In this moving collection of original psalms, poet Joan Metzner invites us to attend to the enlivening Spirit of God within and to write our own words of truth, hope, and longing from the depths of our personhood. Convinced that there is a psalmist within each of us, Metzner encourages writing without fear and with abondonment. Her personal psalm journal is a rich resource for persons seeking to deepen their spiritual lives."

Dr. Colleen M. Griffith
Institute of Religious Education and Pastoral Ministry
Boston College

"*Plucking the Strings* achieves its goal of helping readers quiet down to listen to the stirrings of the heart and then to celebrate the psalm/songs found there. Following the suggestions made by the author at the end of each chapter, readers become troubadours of their own experience.

"Sr. Joan dares to open herself before us. In the directness of her poetry, she does not hide her pain, nor does she hoard her joy. She calls us to do the same with the challenge, 'Remember who you are.' The psalmist within each of us has an opportunity to emerge and take its rightful place among the poets of the spirit."

Jo-Ann Iannotti, O.P.
Wisdom House, Retreat & Conference Center
Litchfield, CT

Plucking the Strings...

A Personal PSALM Journal

JOAN METZNER

XXIII
TWENTY-THIRD PUBLICATIONS
Mystic, CT 06355

Twenty-Third Publications
185 Willow Street
P.O. Box 180
Mystic, CT 06355
(860) 536-2611
800-321-0411

ISBN 0-89622-733-2
Library of Congress Catalog Card Number 97-60533
Printed in the U.S.A.

Dedication

I would like to dedicate this book to my Maryknoll Community, as well as to all the psalmists in my life, budding and full-fledged. Thank you for bringing out the psalmist in me.

Acknowledgments

Thank you for your support and encouragement: Marcella Hoesl, M.M., you first prompted me to seek out publishers for my writings.

Richard Marie McKinney, M.M., you have offered wit and wise critique along the way.

Jo-Ann Iannotti, O.P., you labored through the first form of this book with me.

And to you, some of many friends who have faithfully journeyed with me along this path:

Nancy, Don, Mary Ellen, Hallie, Ken, Ric, Mary Lou, Rosie, Miriam, Veronica, Stephanie, and Grace.

Contents

Psalm Starters

A Personal Psalm Journal

Introduction

We are all psalmists.

The word "psalm," is taken from a Greek word meaning "a plucking of strings." Its root is in the same word as "psaltery," an ancient stringed instrument plucked by fingers or a plectrum. Our own psaltery within is waiting to be plucked. The inner critic, that judgmental voice inside, may try to convince us that we can't do this. But with a bit of a nudge, we can release the psalmist within and set the strings of our heart stirring.

This book is meant to be that nudge. Each of us is a book of the Bible waiting to be written; maybe an Acts of the Apostles, a book of Lamentations, a book of Job, a book of Joan, a book of Sarah, a book of Tom, the Gospel according to Jim, to Betty, to Grace. Our story is a scripture, a revelation of God's mercy and faithfulness.

The psalmist within is seeking expression. Don't restrict yourself by writing what you think you should, but tell God or Jesus or Mary or your Higher Power what is really on your mind and in your heart. Don't mince words. As a participant in a poetry gathering said, "Write without shame."

Since it is with the ear—both the inner ear and the outer ear—that we hear or feel the stirrings, I sometimes image a large ear, even draw an ear to help me focus. Psalming is an adventure where we "play by ear." We ask God to lend us an ear and God asks the same of us.

Use the book as a starter and let your free spirit take over. If you need more space for your writing, find a notebook or some paper to use along with this book. You may want to use drawings or photos or news clippings to illustrate your work. And you may want to turn on some music and dance, or sing and chant your own psalm.

The psalms in this book have come from my heart and from my experience. They echo many of the same thoughts and emotions that you too may have felt at one time or another. In some of the psalms, I have imagined a response from God to my own prayer. These psalm sections, my sense of God's words, are in italics.

Launch out into the deep, into the depths of your heart, where "deep calls unto deep." You may want to use this book while on a retreat day or on a longer period of solitude. Or you could use it as your morning prayer time. Start at the beginning or go wherever you feel led to explore the book.

Choose a focal phrase or word from the psalms that are given here to spark your own. Or select a phrase that comes to you and repeat it often during the day. If your work or living situation allows, you could pray your psalm at noon time, in the late afternoon, evening, and before going to bed at night. Perhaps you could use your psalms in a communal way, as well.

Preparing to Pluck the Strings

Slow down and become attentive. The word "attentive" means to wait...expect...to give heed...to consider...to stretch toward. In our society it's not always easy to slow down and attend. But there are a variety of practices to help us do just that. I'd like to share a few with you.

Breathing: Inhale deeply from the diaphragm. Exhale, sighing a bit. Do this very slowly. You can observe your breath with your mind's eye as you do this. Or, you may count to five as you inhale and exhale. Become present to the moment, to yourself. Breathe in the light and joy and peace of God, and breathe out all the noises and mistakes and distractions. Sigh well.

Music: Perhaps you have a tape of music that you find particularly helpful in relaxing and becoming calm. There are also relaxation tapes available which many people find helpful. Sing your own song aloud.

Candle: Slowly and attentively light a candle. Sit and watch it flicker and burn. Reflect on how you, too, are a candle. The Spirit within burns away our "wick-edness," and fills our whole being with light.

Pictures: Display a favorite picture or photograph that calms you and brings happy thoughts. I have a lovely picture of the Good Shepherd whispering into the ear of the sheep as he caresses it which puts me into a peaceful way.

Dance or Gestures: You may do this in rhythm with breathing, if you wish. Choose gestures of offering, as in cupped hands. Lift up all your fears, loves, hates, guilts toward God.

Postures: Various traditions suggest a variety of postures. Sitting upright in a comfortable chair is a good way to focus your energy and relax your mind. Some people prefer to lie down on the floor. Choose a posture that is comfortable for you.

Crying: Sometimes we just need to cry in order to return to our place of peace.

Walk: Take a short walk to clear your head and refresh your heart. Or take a longer walk and reflect on the words of your psalm, and the feelings in your heart.

Beginning to psalm

As you become still and quiet with God or your Guide, start to write out what is on your mind and in your heart. The biblical psalmists were not shy about writing and sharing their innermost thoughts and feelings—holy or unholy—about God or their neighbor, so we should feel free to do the same.

Write: just do it. Write without shame. You can keep your words privately in your notebook and scribble and cartoon and cross out—whatever. Don't be inhibited by a blank piece of paper. Just pour out your thoughts and feelings. Sometimes I expect to compose a profound psalm, with brilliant images and words, and all that comes is something like, "It hurts." So I stay with that feeling or find a place to sigh very loudly.

If distractions come, write them down as part of your psalm, or in another place. Let them be as clouds that you note and let gently pass, then return to your mind and heart.

Carry your prayer throughout the day with an antiphon from your psalm. An antiphon is a response, an answer. Your antiphon can be a way to stay in touch with your psalm throughout the day. Choose a phrase or word or verse which resounds with you. Chew on it, ruminate with it, let it surround you, become you. Make it into a melody. Put it into the pocket of your heart for use during the day. Let it stay on your lips.

Here are some examples of antiphons:

Thank you for rooting me in your compassion, O God!
Thank you for rooting me in your compassion.

Doubt not my mercy, dear heart,
Doubt not my mercy.

Your love is stronger than death, O God.
Your love endures forever.

You are my everlasting light, O God.
You are my light forever.

Wait for wisdom; wait for wisdom.

Wisdom spirit, come to me.
Wisdom spirit, come to me.

I trust in you forever, O God.
I trust in you forever.

You can also use phrases from the biblical Psalms as antiphons for prayer. Here are some of my favorite verses:

Psalm 9:1
I will give thanks to God with all my heart;
I will tell of all your wonderful deeds.

Psalm 25:4
Make me know your ways, O God;
Teach me your paths.

Psalm 27:1
God is my Light and Salvation.
Whom shall I fear?

Psalm 31:24

Be strong and let your heart be bold
All you who hope in God.

Psalm 57:7

My heart is steadfast, O God,
My heart is ready.

Psalm 131:1

O God, my heart is not lifted up,
My eyes are not raised too high.

Psalm 131:2

As a little child on the lap of its mother.
As a little child, so is my soul within me.

Stay with your antiphon and psalm for as long as it stirs your heart. If you have time during the day, pray your psalm. And in the evening go to bed with it in your heart.

If you reach a point of deep awareness of God's presence, forget this book and these ideas. Simply revel in the knowledge that "God is."

Each moment is a chance to psalm to God, an opportunity to pluck the strings, a time to call upon your antiphon. Welcome to the world of psalming. I promise you a rewarding adventure!

PSALMING

Have you ever spent time reveling in the act of being, appreciating life, your life? Let this psalm lead you to that place.

I Am

There are no words, my God.
There are no words.
Only amazement
only joy
that I am what I am.
Only gratitude that you have created me
cared for me
and called me by name.

I am...
You have given life to me,
unioned me with all the living,
with all the ideas
springing forth from you,
fountain of life.

I am...
and I will always be
in life with you,
in love with you.

The wonder of it all—
I am.

Take time to simply be with God. How does this feel?

Nature can sometimes speak to us of God. Let it pluck your strings as you read this psalm.

Break Through

Surge through the churning waters,
O dolphins of the seas.
Break through the illusions of passing clouds,
O rising sun.

Show us the flight to freedom,
O birds of the sky.
Speak to us of God's strength,
O trees of the earth.

Jupiter, Sun, and Saturn,
You entice our minds.
Moon, Mars, and Venus,
you captivate our curiosity.

O God, all creation is mute
in your presence.
All is nothing but miniscule molecules...
nothing, only nothing.

Creation fades; it withers and dies.
But you remain forever,
O beloved God of my heart.
You remain forever.

Break through your shells,
O children of the earth.
Break through your shells
and come to me.

After dwelling with this psalm, let some aspect of nature touch you. Then start writing...don't think too much, just write.

Are you aware of the cages in your life that keep you from flying free? What are the bars in your relationships?

Cages

Step out of your cage.
Rage no longer in your confinement.
Only let the Spirit
direct you to freedom.

Be cagey no more
but soar, soar.
Play among the stars,
and run to the dawn.

Gauge not the journey-time
beyond today.
But let sage words deliver you
from definitions
that bar your way to living...
just this stage,
just this page of life.

Wage not war with your oppressors
but release them from their cages
so that all will be free to soar.

Ask God for the key to the cages that keep your real self locked up. With all confidence, write your holy (or not so holy) thoughts and feelings about your cages.

Are you afraid to face your hidden hates and secret sins? This psalm may help you to turn to Mary and confide these to her.

Mary

Daughter of the dawn,
you have broken into my life
with your gentle presence,
with your merry spirit.

You never chide,
but invite me
to confide to you
my hidden hates
and secret sins,
fears, tears, and all.

I call upon you
with faith
in your faithfulness.
You coach me,
you comfort me,
you fill my mind
with your presence.

Thank you for your gift of glee.
Thank you for your playfulness.
Thank you for revealing yourself to me,
Daughter of the Dawn.

What is Mary's role in your life? Speak to her, sing to her, write to her from your heart.

Is there some area in your life where you feel the need of Wisdom? In your family, work or other relationships? In finding your passion?

Waiting

I wait for Wisdom,
my sister Spirit.
I wait for her comforting word.
With vigilance I watch
the movements of my heart;
with patience, the feelings of my body;
with gentleness, the wanderings of my mind.

With the dawn, I sense her presence,
squeezing my hand.
massaging my shoulder,
embracing me with total understanding,
bestowing deepest wisdom.

I welcome her smile
as I relax
and feel my own smile
creasing my face.
My whole being makes merry
because she knows—
and now I know—
that indeed, all is well.

Let the quiet mood of this psalm move you to write to the Spirit of Wisdom for help in sensing her presence and hearing her word.

Sometimes, when a loved one has died, grief and pain can take over our thoughts. But there is another perspective to death that illuminates God's presence.

Death

I went to the cemetery
to pay respect
to the memory of my loved ones.

The stones needed some attention.
And so I went to work
clearing away the dirt and weeds
from the stones.

"How dark it must be down deep," I thought.
But a light came, and
it dawned on me:

"I am not a body. I am free.
I am still as God created me."

And the words echoed
and the depths rumbled:

"I am not a body. I am free.
I am still as God created me."

A repetitive chant,
joyous proclamation
from the heavens, above and within:

"I am not a body. I am free.
I am still as God created me."

Back and forth the words
fill the cemetery,
resound around the cosmos.
The dead engage the living
in a message of radical urgency:

"I am not a body. I am free.
I am still as God created me."

How do you feel about death?

What are your distractions? What takes you away from being mindful during the day, from attention to the voice of God?

Attention

Be attentive
all you distant lands.
Be attentive
children of God.
Be attentive to your Creator
as God is attentive to you.

Listen to the music of the Holy One,
a song of peace,
and learn that
we are wholly one;
we are in communion forever.

Stay with the music of your soul.
Tend to the busy-ness that blocks
the experience of your music.

Let go the thoughts
that prick you with guilt,
that strangle you with worry.
Be gentle with yourself.

Dare to stop the anxiety.
Risk the leap to laughter,
for you are of God, in God.

All your worries are groundless,
all your fears unjustified,
all your discords silly.

God awaits in patience,
infinite patience.
Be attentive to the present moment.

Attend to God's gentle reminders of infinite love. Listen to what God is saying to you, and your response.

Are you afraid of being honest with God? With others? Maybe you doubt God's compassion and forget that God does not take offense.

Anger

My heart was filled with the cacophony of anger.
Rage enveloped me like a violent storm.
Vindication churned within.
Guilt surfaced and disheartened me.

You were far away and you seemed angry, too.
But I turned to you, my God.
I became attentive
and in my distress I confided to you
my hidden hates, my angry rebellion.

And you anointed me with your mercy.
Yes, you adapted to me.
You put Spirit-notes on my tongue.
I heard the music of the dawn in my heart.

No longer would I flee from your wrath.
You stilled the wind and the storm.
You brought peace to my awareness.
You healed me to see that the holiness in me
is one with the holiness that is you.

You took a competitive spirit from my heart,
a spirit that would have me see myself
as "holier than thou,"
or as a victim.

You brought your Spirit to our relationship
and gave me peace.

Write in total honesty about your angry feelings toward God and others. God's response may surprise you.

Crying can be a healing part of life. Absorb these words and let them touch you.

Crying

My heart is crying, O God,
my heart is crying.
I am deceived by earthly illusions.
I am as one who is blind to truth.

I hear of genocide
and persecution in the world,
floods, earthquakes, other natural disasters.

I see theft and murder
right down the street…
the grocer in the South End,
the baby in the West End.

I struggle to confide to you
my secret sins and hidden hates:
could it be that they perpetuate the conflict?

Give attention, distant lands!
Listen, cities, farms, and suburbs!

I will never punish you.
I will never forsake you.
I will never hold your "sin" against you.

You think you are separated from me.
But I tell you this can never be.
You think you are separated from each other,
brother and sister no more.

Yet you are the refugee:
You are the flood victim,
the grocer, the child,
the murderer, the thief,
You are also the relief worker;
the journalist, the doctor,
the military.

You have an irreplaceable role in the world.
Choose forgiveness,
for your forgiveness means peace
for all your brothers and sisters.

I will never condemn you.
for you are of me
and I can never annihilate myself.
Choose forgiveness,
for my justice is mercy
and mercy is my nature.

Cry no more, my beloved,
Cry no more.

Explode with the cries of your heart and the cries of the world. Let the Spirit lead you to new spaces.

Where is the violence in your life? Does it seem to come from within or without?

Violence

Our minds are bombarded, my God,
with news, information,
commercials, billboards.
More and more messages assail our world.

We are plagued with the locusts
of violent thoughts that eat away at us.
How can peace prevail, my God?
How can peace prevail?

Break through the barrier of attacks,
my dear ones,
as a chick patiently pecks through
to new birth.
Be willing to pass through misty clouds
to a mountain of the unknown.
Slow down...
slow down and regain your rhythms.

Let the noise
and the chatter and the clatter
scatter before the coming
of the Spirit of stillness,
who gently breaks into your life
as the dawn heralds a new day.

Keep yourself in sweet remembrance
of the sun/Sonrise.
Know that peace will prevail
for peace is our inheritance.

Let your own experience of violence find expression in a psalm.

Do you sometimes feel frustrated that you don't know what true justice is? This psalm takes us back to our origins, where justice originates.

Justice

O God, my God,
your ways are beyond
our understanding.

The earth and all it contains,
the stars and planets,
the dawning suns of the universe
are not what they seem.
They are but
mocking molecules of nothingness.

This world, this universe,
stretches the limits of imagination.
Yet all is nothing.

Only you, our Source,
our Wellspring,
exceed our worlds,
our words,
for you are infinite Mystery
who knows only of oneness,
just oneness.

In quiet revolution
we turn back to our beginnings,
back to our awareness of you, our God,
whom we have never really left,
doing just this...just this.

Back to you
our author and origin...
back to you,
our justice and peace.

Write from and about your real self, the real presence springing from your originality. Do justice to yourself.

Do you sometimes forget the comfort that comes from abiding with God? What blocks your awareness of this peace?

Abode

I will abide with you today, O God,
in silence of mind and heart.
Be my abode.
I will rest in the certitude that
love never condemns.
You are at my side.

Abide, yes abide with Me.
I would converse with you,
listen to your story
as you calm your mind
from vain pursuits.

Abide. Yes, abide with Me.
I would remind you
to choose again.
I would invite you
to tenderly care
for that frightened child.
I would draw you from
a fruitless path
to show you
the comfort of my way.

Abide. Yes, abide with Me.

Feel God's desire to abide in your awareness. Describe this feeling. What is it like to have God abide in you?

Plucking the strings of our stories sometimes leads us to dance, sing, or act out in other physical ways. As you sit with this psalm let it move you to your own unique expression.

Dancing

You have revealed your faithfulness,
my Creator.
I will dance in the dawn
of your revelation.
I will rejoice in your mercies.
I will exult in your gracious name.

As moments of our lives touch,
as our stories weave in and out
I look to you for the final chapter,
the ultimate revelation,
the whole story.

I give thanks to you
for keeping company with me.
I give thanks to you,
Source of my life.
I give thanks to you,
Spirit of my being.
I give thanks for you,
living God.

Write your feelings about this psalm. Express—don't repress—what impresses you. Let your pen dance on the paper.

How do you experience the Word of God? What does it do for you? Where do you find it?

Your Word

Your Word, O Lord, is food for thought,
a eucharistic moment.
Its healing powers soothe my mind.

Your Word awakens me from my dream
to communion with all God's people.
Your Word, O Lord,
helps me shed the skin of my false self
as it sheds light on my true self.

Your Word whispers
in a gentle breeze.
In it, silence resounds
throughout the endless distances
of the universe.
It reverberates within my being,
giving joy to my heart.

Your Word is a gentle correction
for my mistakes,
a tender touch to my confusion,
strengthening wine for my spirit,
nourishing bread for my soul.

Your Word exchanges grace for my doubt,
favor for my sense of unworthiness.
It puts me in contact with you,
my Alpha and Omega,
my Beginning and End.
Your Word is play

for my inner child.
It tickles her funnybone,
dazzles her imagination
and delights her inner eye.

Your Word is revelation, enthusiasm.
Your Word presides at the Last Supper.
Your Word is forever.

Take one insight from this psalm that touches you and write it down. Play with the words; let them echo your own thoughts, your own images of God's Word.

Psalms can take us to our inner sanctum, where a sense of the sacred is revealed. Let that sense take over as you chant, "Sanctus, sanctus, sanctus...holy, holy, holy."

Sanctus

Sanctus...sanctus...sanctus.
Spirit chant stirring in midnight darkness
resounding in the silence of my soul,
profound pulsating peace.

Sanctus...sanctus...sanctus.

Hymn of heavenly "hosts"
stirs the earth:
welcome, brother and sister,
communioned in the same sanctus spirit,
sharing breath and bread.

Sanctus...sanctus...sanctus.

Blessed is the one coming
in the name of the Lord,
proclaiming:
Sanctus...sanctus...sanctus.

Jesus, Mary, Joseph,
Gandhi, Maura, Ita,
Nancy, Don, Mary Ellen,
coming in the name of the Lord,
proclaiming:
Sanctus...sanctus...sanctus.

From eternity to eternity the cadence continues...
SANCTUS...SANCTUS...SANCTUS.

Sing out your holy images. In peacefulness and with gentle love write your own sanctus, your hymn of holy awareness.

How have you experienced God's closeness to you? God's promises of security?

Security

In God is my security.
In God I trust.
I will have no fear.

For I am faith-fastened to my Creator,
securely stitched,
woven into God's name,
never, ever to be separated.

God has secured me,
assured me that I am very holy,
always a holy child of God,
always approved.

Rest secure in my promises,
for you are beloved of me.

Leap from the trap
that would have you think
that you are a failure,
a sinner, a "bad" person.

Leap in faith to me,
for I am your security.
Rejoice in
my irresistible love
for you.
Have trust in me as
I have trust in you.

Let me carry you through the woods
when it is dark,
for I can never fail you.
I can never let you go.

I am your security now
and every moment
into a promise fulfilled
and celebrated
world without end.

Reflect on what makes you feel secure. Offer your anxiety and insecurity about your life to God in a celebration of thankfulness and joy.

Psalms are not meant to be a task of speed reading. Read this once, then go back and pause…savor…ruminate.

My Smile

The dawn has come.
I will smile in its light,
smile at my mistakes,
my second guessing,
my anger, my fear.

The dawn has come.
I will smile in its light,
smile at my grief, my guilt,
my anxiety, my tears.

The dawn has come.
I will smile in its light,
smile at the dictator and the prisoner,
the saint, the sinner.

The dawn has come.
I will smile in its light,
smile at my past,
my struggles, my story.

The dawn has come.
I will smile in its light,
smile at the grocer,
the mail carrier,
the German shepherd next door,
my friends, my foes.

The dawn has come.
I will smile in its light.

Use the antiphon as your own and smile as you write your own words in between the lines. Let the antiphon stay with you during the day. Chant it or say it in a comfortable rhythm.

What happens to you when you turn to God? Stand and put your hands over your eyes. Slowly turn in the opposite direction as you remove your hands from your eyes. What did you experience?

God's Smile

I have turned to God
and God has lifted me up.
I have run to my God
and God has embraced me.
As a mother tends to her little child
so God has comforted me.

God has smiled upon me
and I have been saved.
The Spirit of compassion
has softly laughed within me
and that has made all the difference.

I will confide to God
the worries and anxieties of my heart
and they will be transformed.
Yes, I will find God's ear
and whisper into it
the secrets of my soul.

I will open my being as a book
before my Creator
and I will wait for Wisdom
to speak.

"Be at peace," come the words,
"for Love does not condemn."

Stay at my side, dear Spirit of strength,
all through the daylight.
Shelter me during the night shadows
and I will echo your smile
forever and ever.

Stay with the message from your psalming. Let it quiet you during the day or energize you. Relax with it when the day seems to get out of control.

When do you take yourself too seriously? Do you find a particular image or word helpful as you try to put it in perspective? What helps you to see the silliness of it all?

Silly

My feelings nag me
my thoughts accuse me,
yet I will smile
at their silliness,
Compassionate Mother,
for you are ever with me.

I will trust in your favor.
I will heed your words.
As a parade of thoughts
come to pass in my mind,
I will just say, "Boo!"
to the ego
for its ragings are powerless
and its silly antics
a tiny mouse
roaring at the universe.

Write about the parade of thoughts in your life. Which thoughts and feelings nag you? Can you hear the tiny mouse that accuses you with a "roar" at the universe, your universe? Fill your page with silliness.

What is the source of your joy? What keeps it from surfacing? You may find the answer in this psalm.

Laughter

Come, let us join in the lightness of God.
Let us listen to God's healing humor.

Contagious be our giggles
as little children indulge in silliness.

The rains proclaim the life of God,
the fruits of the earth, God's abundance.

But we will outlive
the earth and its oceans.
We will enter into the laughter of God
and smile at passing illusions.

So chuckle, little brooks,
gurgle, rollicking rivulets.

Rumble with joy, all you mountains.
In rustling music, lift up your leaves,
you trees of the world.

City and suburb, villages and jungles,
farmers, nomads, nurses, and mechanics,
politicians, doctors, teachers, and trash collectors,
release your serious burdens for an instant
and enter together into the spirit of joviality.

Laugh at your fears of God and one another
and let peace and justice
softly rain on the earth.

Write of God's lightheartedness as you see your Source in a new light. Be ready to call upon God to share the saving grace of a kindly humor today.

Silent times provide an ambiance where we can learn to enjoy the Spirit, as she speaks in a gentle breeze.

Silence

In the silence of your heart
I will speak to you, my beloved.
In the silence of your heart.

Gently let pass
your fears and hates;
wait...
for your beloved in silence.

Return to the tabernacle
the tent within where dwells
My holy Spirit
your holy Spirit.

Absorb the silence.
Absorb the Spirit.
Absorb the joy.

For that is my covenant with you
now and forever.

Do you enjoy silence? If not, what interferes with this enjoyment? Write to your beloved Spirit of God about this.

Are you afraid of love? Afraid to let God's limitless love into your limited world? Let this psalm take you into the deeper areas of your heart, where God's tender gaze meets your yearning for love.

Open Heart

O God, my God,
my heart is open before you.
In peaceful silence
deep calls unto deep.
Laser-like, your light
heals my hates, my hurts,
my secret sins.
I will delight in your mercy.

I will revel in your magnificence
for you companion me
in the darkness.
You confirm me in my holiness.
You reveal your presence
in holy instants.
I rejoice in your
revelations.
I exult in your holy name.

Open your heart to God and as you write about what is there, invite God's healing, laser-like light to penetrate your whole being.

You don't have to wait until you are perfect to start psalming. You only have to be honest about where you are at in your life.

Conversion

I wandered far from you,
my beloved.
I wandered far, or so it seemed.

I hid behind bushes,
sought refuge in caves
went to faraway places.

My heart sought peace
in sundry spaces,
entered into human races.

And all the while
your smile eluded me.
I took it all so seriously
until one day it dawned on me:
I'm found forever, for eternity.
And your laughter entered into me.

And now I know conversion comes
a thousand times a day
as I awaken to a lighter way
and come out of hiding to a world of play.
Past nightmarish schemes to happy dreams,
embraced by my beloved.

The dawning of benevolence
comes a thousand times a day.

Write from your hiding places, then write from your "finding" places, as you express your real self to God.

Do you find hints of God's presence during the day? An insight that comes while driving the car or taking a walk or waiting in line?

God's Voice

The groaning earth
the shimmering stars
the silent skies
only hint at your mystery, O God.

Playful, bantering friends,
irresistible, charming children,
experienced, wise elders,
reveal your benediction, O God.

Our world speaks of separation…
insane separation.

Yet if I give ear
I will hear
the voice of God
rustling in the leaves
stirring in the breeze
breathing in the seas
playfully teasing my mind
gently seizing my heart
in a miracle of communion.

Which words touch you in this psalm? Expand on them and tuck them into your heart to remind you of God during the day.

As you pause with this psalm, open yourself to God's vision of you. God has blessed vision, beatific vision and would have us see the same way.

Who You Are

You are the pupil of my eye
the delight of my heart.

Remember who you are.

You are my treasure,
immeasurable joy to me,
a constant source of holiness.

Remember who you are.

You are my offspring,
beloved self of my Self,
name of my Name,
reality of my Reality.

Remember who you are.

You are a star,
carrier of my light,
radiant in my sight.

Remember who you are.

You are my missioner,
ordained to forgive as I forgive,
to confirm my presence
in your life,
and in the lives of your brothers and sisters.

Ordained to lift up your heart,
the hearts of all my children,
one in the glory of our spirit.

Ordained to learn justice
and make peace.

Remember who you are.

How does God see you? Write some of the names God gives to you and the mission that flows from each name. Take one of them with you into the day.

Comparisons with others' thoughts and writings can pull you off course. As you go into this psalm appreciate yourself in all your uniqueness and at the same time your oneness in the Spirit.

Differences

Star differs from star,
flower from flower,
person from person.

Points of view abound
preferences resound
insights found
from day to day.

And you, O Lord our God,
delight in the differences.

You are the merriment
of silent spaces,
creator of a thousand faces.

You behold us in rapt attention
and your Spirit hovers
until we are no longer
threatened by disagreements;
unlike we, like you,
delight in the differences.

And then, there are no differences.

How do you see your uniqueness? Your differences? Write down the feelings that both yours and others' uniqueness and differences stir up in you.

Psalming takes us to our roots. Feel yourself rooted in your chair or on the floor. As you tend to the psalm, feel yourself rooted in God's compassion.

Tree

As a tree rooted deep in the earth,
whose toes reach down for living waters
whose branches stretch
to the heavens,
so is my soul rooted in your mercy,
O God.

Your mercy is my comfort by day,
my security by night.
Your mercy is my strength.
It encompasses the depths
of my suffering
the heights of my joy.
It adapts to every mood,
fits into every need.
Your mercy fills the earth
with compassion.
My heart rejoices in your care for us.

Tend to your tree,
my beloved gardener.
Make me safe in your mercy forever.

And I will never doubt you,
for your faithfulness
is ultimately irresistible.

Stay with your rootedness. Let your pen give expression to the experience of your body and heart.

Do you sometimes feel at a loss for words, in a space where you seem far from home? With people, but not really at one?

Longing

I feel not at home
on this planet, O God.
I feel not at home.

My mind wanders, wonders
where you are.
I know not the meaning of this.
I know not the meaning of that.
But I know it is not here
I find my home.

Hear your child who calls upon you,
who longs for you
with ardent desire,
pulled in distant directions,
dulled by a dozen distractions.

I know not how to draw near to you.
I know not your name.
Speak to my heart.

My beloved child,
My Holy Spirit is in you.
Your home is nowhere, but everywhere.
Your Savior is within and without.

I will transform your tears
into living waters
to satisfy you forever.

I will transform malicious words
and ill intent
into the twitter of sparrows,
into clouds of nothingness.

I will teach you to live
in the present moment.
I will give you a glimpse of home
a spirit of adventure.

In that peaceful place of "I don't know"
You will relish a glimmer of glory.
You will savor a sample of the banquet.
You will catch an instant of home.

Return to the sacred silence where I am.
Rejoice that my name
is in your heart,
in the silence of your heart.

Be still and know that
I am your God, your spirit,
your Savior.

Write from your own homeless space, and find a message for your heart for the day.

Have you ever felt a yearning to be as free as a skylark? Be grateful for those moments and walk with the following psalm (or your own psalm) on your lips.

Home

Where is my home, O God,
where is my home?
Over valley and hill
have I roamed.
I have roamed
yearning always
to be skylark free,
to return to thee,
to return to thee.

Spirit guide,
you amaze, you amuse.
You never refuse.

You never refuse
to direct my feet
in the way of peace,
to bring release,
to bring release
to my yearning soul,
alone, so alone.

I'm on my way home.
Yes, on my way home.

Converse with God about your yearnings, your homelessness, your moments of skylark freedom.

As you praise God through the psalm, stay with the images it evokes in you.

Praise

Praise God with toasts and tickertape.
Praise God with the sounds of the horn.
With dancing come into God's presence,
heralding birth of new morn.

No longer our fears will haunt us.
No more must I cower in shame.
For God has revealed our salvation;
revel in God's holy name.

Praise our Creator with cymbals,
with Japanese flute and trombones,
with African drums and guitars,
clap your hands as we all journey home.

Our hearts exult in creation,
in the God who has given us breath,
who promises life without ending,
who has taken the sting out of death.

Your psalm need not rhyme. Simply find images of life today which you can use to give praise to God.

Have you ever felt that you were falling, and no one was there to catch you? Did God provide someone to help you? Go slowly and gently into this psalm.

Catch Me

Why, O Lord, why
did you turn from me
and not hear my cry?
Why, O Lord, why?

I kept on calling,
afraid I was falling from your favor.

I thought you were out to get me,
to catch me in the act...
But you assured me
that I was safe,
for you would always be there
to catch me
if I felt that I was falling.

You saved me from the grave
and brought me into the lightness
of a new creation,
stirred by your contagious laughter.

You caught me again and again
and re-minded me
every time
I fell for the line
of empty promises
I could count on you
to catch me.

Confidently talk to God about your fears of falling, your cries for help, and be ready for a surprising response.

After you have read this psalm, slowly breathe the antiphon in and out. Reflect on new beginnings in your life.

Morning

At the dawn of day
—a quiet time called morning—
a peaceful being,
greater than I
breathed life
into my nostrils
and whispered,
"My child is pure and holy as I am."

I listened,
but I couldn't believe.
Again and again the ritual continued
until one beautiful morning
I woke up and understood.
I offered myself
to receive the breath
and the word,
"My child is pure and holy as I am."

And now I know
creation comes
a thousand times a day,
again and again,
breath after breath after breath.
And I find my heart saying
to that peaceful being,
"I'd like to spend eternity with you."

"My child is pure and holy as I am." What feelings does this antiphon inspire in you? Remind yourself of these feelings to help you during the day.

Sometimes, even the best relationships can tear us apart, set us off-course. When you feel rejected or your world is falling apart, know that you are not alone.

Off-Course

God, where are you?
I'm pulled in all directions
to achieve and produce,
by those who would make me feel guilty
who push my buttons,
ignite my anxiety, my fear, my anger.

Dear friends are dying;
I miss them.
My tears bathe my face
with sadness,
the day is overcast.
Will the sun never shine again?

My limitations taunt me.
My friends reject me.
My ego mocks and points a
bony finger at me.
My face is cast down to earth.
Where is relief?

Thank God for friends
who return me to stillness,
who help me to
bare my heart
who point me in the right direction
along the pathways of peace.

Thank God for lifting me up,
for sending someone to comfort me,
to counsel me,
to cause me to laugh again,
to restore the Sonrise to my life.

Don't mince words. Tell God where you are at, what you think of your "friends," even what you think of God. Leave room for God to reply after you get it out of your system.

Do you ever wonder where you are going in life, what it is you are called to do, or be?

Mission

God, God of my life,
what is my mission?
Where is my mission?
Where are you?

Put aside your misgivings,
spend time with me,
rest in unknowing.
Sit with me.
Walk with me
until you feel peace,
emanating from within,
freeing you from fear.

You feel that you need to produce,
to fit into a definition,
a "role" as others see it,
as you see it.
Put this aside;
abide...only abide with me.

Spend time doing nothing.
Defy your own definitions,
categories, titles.
Only be my child,
my beautiful one,
my dearest Joan.
Accomplish nothing. Plan nothing.
Know nothing,
except peace that comes from me,
your God.

Ask God for direction. Plot out the journey through your own psalm, in your own words inspired by God.

If we are rooted in God's mercy, our nightmares and fears will be transformed into unending joy.

Mercy

My soul is rooted in your mercy, O God.
Prophets tell of your anger,
your just anger.
"Vengeance is yours," they say.
But that is a false god,
a god of spite.
My soul comes from a God of mercy.
My soul is rooted in your mercy, O God.

Where are the prophets who tell
of your irresistible love;
your irresistible faith in us?
My soul is rooted in your mercy, O God.

I am jealous, O God.
I hate my competitors.
I seek punishment for murderers.
And all the while
there is murder in my heart...
there is mercy in your heart, O God.
My soul is rooted in your mercy, O God.

Sleep for a while, my child,
until you are ready to awaken
to the truth you proclaim:
Your soul is rooted in my mercy.

I will transform your nightmares
into happy dreams,
because your soul is rooted in my mercy.

I am your Maker, your Author.
I can never abandon you;
I can never uproot you.
Nothing can separate you
from the deep union of your life.
Not earthquake, tornado,
nor the fires of hell.
For my love has promised you an awakening,
a breakthrough for all people.
because your soul is rooted in my mercy.

You will feel the joy of my compassion,
the surging exultation of living waters
filling your being
because your soul is rooted in my mercy
forever.

Where and how have you experienced God's mercy in your life? Where do you most need to feel God's mercy now?

What do you feel and think when you see a baby in its mother's lap? What does this psalm say to you?

Peace Child

I have no profound insights tonight,
no startling revelations.
I have only your profound silence;
I am your peace child.

I have let go of the struggle
to be more special,
always right,
always thinking of you.

I no longer take guilt as my guide.
I have chosen you, Mother of peace,
as my partner,
your sweet silence as my food,
my communion,
my eucharist.

I relish your serenity,
dear Mother,
and your laughing silence.

I welcome your stillness;
I am quiet.
No false gods do I choose,
but a God who is blissfully happy,
who inSpirits me
to rejoice in our common destiny.

Goodnight, dear Mother,
I am your peace child.

Let this psalm nudge you to pour out your thoughts about a loving God who watches over us, as a mother does her peaceful child.

What kind of feelings do you have when you have to say, "I don't know?"

Know Nothing

I know not anything, my God,
I know not anything.

My heart was distressed,
my spirit sad.

I turned to you, my Help,
and you answered me.

"Be still and know nothing,"
you counseled.
"Be still and let me be God."

I fingered my healing beads
and the Mother responded,

"Be still and know nothing.
Be still and let me be Mother."

And the birds chirped
and the hills echoed your silence.

And now my heart grows full
because it knows nothing,
save that it is
promised your Presence
forever.

Write a confession of not knowing, with words that come directly to God's ear from your heart.

Does it hurt again? What hurts? Where does it hurt? See if you identify with this stark cry of pain.

It Hurts

this ache
this pain
this throb
this absence from felicity.

I scream for vision,
for an embrace with truth
that heals

this ache
this pain
this throbbing,
sobbing,
robbery of felicity.

Write out your own cry of pain. Let the words come from your place of hurting.

Kannon is a Japanese expression of the Goddess of mercy. Her face is serene and she has elongated ears, symbolizing the meaning of her name, that is, "the one who hears the cries of the world."

Who Hears?

Who hears these silent sighs,
sobbing cries of earth...
these eruptions of pain
vain in their fierce desperation
to find understanding?

No words,
only cries
in a cacophony,
a symphony of anguish.

Where is God?

Has God no ears
to hear my screams
to understand
my nightmarish dreams of grief?

Has God no heart
to attend
to the moans of earth
groaning in the pangs
of giving birth to a new labor?

Where are your sighing cries to the One who hears?

How do you find your way back when you have gone off-course?

Recourse

When your thoughts
take you off-course
have recourse to me.

Choose again to remember me,
without guilt, without fretting,
without getting into a frenzy.

Only say my name
and you will become aware
that I am there for you.

Simply say my name
and I will return you to yourself.
When you run to me
I will embrace you.

I will show you your function.
When you reconsider your needs
I will supply them.
When you show
just a little willingness to trust me
I will work wonders in you,
show you
the mighty work of the spirit.

When you confide to me your shadows
I will shine my light upon you
to awaken you
to your holiness.

Enter into conversation with God as your guide at the helm. Share your off-course feelings or situation and have recourse to the one in whom you have faith.

In what areas of life do you want direction? Relationships, work, prayer?

Direct Me

Direct me, Jesus, direct me.

In you I find peace and grace,
the power to choose again.
Real power;
to arise with you and choose
Spirit thoughts,
to return to my God.

Direct me, O Jesus, direct me.

I depend on things outside me
to give me peace.
But you teach me to know
that peace comes from you
and is within.

When I let you help me
undo the layers of guilt and attack,
defense and offense and judgment,
there is peace.
When I look at my unpeacable thoughts
peacefully with you
there is peace.

Direct me, O Jesus, direct me.

I depend on what others think
for my happiness.

But you direct me to think with you,
to put my thoughts and feelings with you,
to witness with you,
to smile with you.

Direct me, O Jesus, direct me.

Write out an intimate conversation with Jesus as your antiphon plays itself and plucks the strings of your heart: "Direct me, O Jesus. Direct me."

Psalming gives us time to lament. What are your personal lamentations?

Lamentation

My beloved Motherland
what is happening to you?
You are feeding your children
competition,
anxiety,
greed, speed, and crack.
And your children suffer
from the lack of nourishment
of a gentle, compassionate lover.

Witness the media
that would manipulate our minds,
the violence
that would destroy our cities,
the leaders
who would hypnotize our brain,
and drug our heart with assertions
that we are on course.

Why are you afraid, little country,
so afraid?

Come back to your roots,
precious people,
and learn
from your spiritual forebears
how to be still,
how to be peaceful
how to find the truth
that will make you free.

Try to express your lamentations with a drawing. How does God respond to your cries?

The Wisdom Spirit takes me back to my home. Bodily and mental diminishment cannot get in the way.

Wisdom Spirit

My body withers
and my thoughts wander,
yet my Spirit stands
strong as the redwoods.
For the Wisdom Spirit herself
is at my side
breathing her being
into my branches,
her life into my leaves.

As her roots reach
down...
down...
down...
deep into the earth,
my soul finds rest
and my heart heads for home.

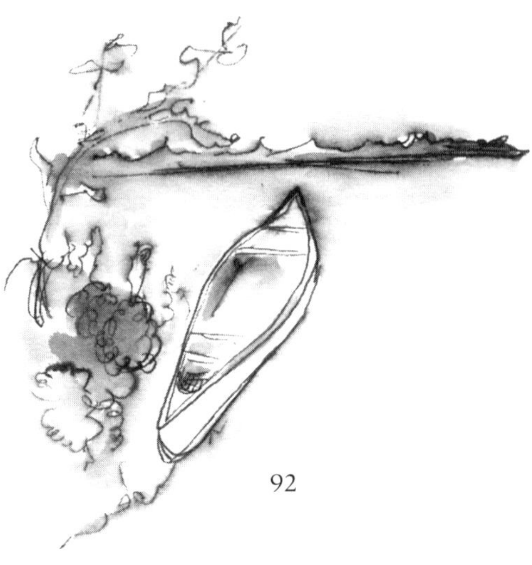

Explore the ways your "withering body and wandering thoughts" respond to the Wisdom Spirit stretching her roots down in your heart.

Do you find your image of Mary changing in your life? How are your challenges similar to hers?

Letting Go

Mary,
you cut the strings
of expectation and control
imposed by the world in which you lived.

You learned how to say
"yes" and "no"
because you dwelt
with the Spirit
in your innermost self.

You even let go
of a mother's attachment to her son,
because your union with him
was deeper than merely physical.

We all have to do
a lot of string-cutting
in this world,
from our first breath of life,
when the umbilical cord is cut
to the last breath of the body,
as our tie to the earth is severed.

When something bothers me too much,
it's time to look at the strings.
I can tighten the reins
and become more and more upset,

or I can loosen the reins,
cut the strings
of expectation and control
and dwell with the Spirit, in Christ.

I, too, can seek counsel
in my innermost self
learning to say
"yes" and "no"
because I have cut the strings
and allowed Jesus and Mary
into my innermost self.

What are the strings that are holding you back? Ask Mary to help you cut them and let go.

Where and when have you experienced the power of Jesus' compassion? As you enter into this psalm embrace the power of true forgiveness, unqualified beyond our limits.

Compassion

Jesus, God, Spirit,
your compassionate love
fills my heart.

When other loves are tenuous,
your love remains
changeless,
limitless,
beyond images.

Your compassion
has conquered suffering,
your love
is stronger than death.

You, Jesus,
joyfully took up your cross.
With a psalm in your heart
you made your way to Calvary,
showing me the overwhelming,
transforming power
of forgiveness.

Love does not condemn but offers forgiveness and compassion. As you write, touch upon new areas of understanding Jesus' relationship to you.

In our efforts to plumb the depths of God, we sometimes falter and fail to experience the mystery of life, that which is beyond all that we see and understand.

Beyond All

Beyond time
as we tell it,
beyond words
as we understand them,
beyond boundaries
we have arbitrarily set up,
pulsates an eternal Energy.

Beyond bodies
as we see them,
beyond symphonies,
as we hear them
beyond events
as we interpret them,
vibrates a Being of unshakeable faith.

In deepest love,
God conceived me
and released me into being;
free, sinless, pure, and holy.
But something in me hesitated
when my Maker said, "Trust me."
And the original harmony
became discordant to my ears.

Lift us beyond all, O God.
Return us to our natural rhythms,
our original harmonies.

Let the sights and sounds of earth
become signs of the Holy Spirit
returning us
to you.

Trust in the mystery of God, the mystery of life. Beyond what—or whom—is this mystery calling you?

PSALM STARTERS

Sometimes one or two words are sufficient to express what is in your heart. Let a word or brief phrase come to your mind, arise from your heart. Allow this word or phrase to stay with you and bring your heart and mind into other places, other ideas.

The psalms which follow on the next few pages use a word or phrase to express a feeling. Let them guide you into response with a written psalm of your own. Or simply be with the thoughts and emotions the word or phrase evokes. Give voice to your soul; let it compose your psalm.

Breathe in God's invitation to love ourselves fully. Inhale love and total acceptance; exhale fear, guilt, and sin.

Be Loved.

Do you feel hesitant about letting yourself be loved? Gently let God expand on the message of these words, perhaps addressing a sense of unworthiness or low self-esteem.

"Thank you" is often a key to God's kingdom. Let your thank you come with a sigh of relief, as you breathe this message in and out.

Thank You.

Have you ever heard our Creator say, "Thank you" to you? Well, God's thanks are with us all the time: all the time! Write your thank you to our source of life and let God whisper a message of gratitude into your ear.

Do you tend to get down on yourself when you make a mistake, when you look at your faults? Yet God sees only the holy in us. Sometimes, a gentle "ooops!" is all that is necessary when we err.

Ooops!

Write out a few of your "ooops" moments and remember during the day to recall the comforting gaze of God.

Do you sometimes think you can handle it all yourself? As you sit with this word, let areas where you may need help today come to the surface.

Help!!

When you are ready, cry out for help. Knowing that you will always be answered, although you may not be prepared to accept the answer in the form in which it comes.

When you spill your orange juice all over the table—or worse—let your initial "Oh, no!" give way to a "Yes!" which weaves through your frustration and anger.

Yes!

Breathe, write, draw, or sing "Yes!" in your own unique way, and let it affirm the astonishing fact of our inseparable union with God and with each other.

As our Inner Sage scribes Wisdom on the pages of our lives, we are ultimately led to respond:

Aha ha ha!

Let your heart choose the Holy Chuckler and scribe your laughter on the pages of your book.

Of Related Interest. . .

Seeking Inner Peace
The Art of Facing Your Emotions
John D. Powers

Have a chat with yourself and discover the hidden you in this fascinating inner dialogue technique. You talk to yourself but when you talk back, you learn who you really are in a new way.
ISBN: 0-89622-344-2, 112 pp, $8.95

Good Morning, Lord
Everyday Prayers for Everyday People
Joseph T. Sullivan

Here are 365 brief, yet thoughtful prayers, one for each day of the year, which deal with ordinary events and feelings as well as those arising from extraordinary situations. They speak to God in everyday language, expressing the joys, hopes, sorrows, disappointments, needs, and concerns common to us all.
ISBN: 0-89622-593-3, 200 pp, $9.95

Songs of Sunrise, Seeds of Prayer
Wayne Simsic

A lovely help to see the Earth as sacred, a teacher of prayer, and a basic way to encounter God. The meditations are wonder-filled and inspiring. Tom Berry notes that Wayne Simsic guides us into a renewal of our primordial intimacy with Earth.
ISBN: 0-89622-600-X, 152 pp, $9.95

Everyday Epiphanies
Seeing the Sacred in Everything
Melannie Svoboda, SND

Offers 175 short stories with topics ranging from the ordinary to the uncommon occasions that we all look forward to and relish when they occur. A comprehensive index cross references topics and themes to stories. ISBN: 0-89622-730-8, 200 pp, $9.95

Available at religious bookstores or from:

TWENTY-THIRD PUBLICATIONS
P.O. Box 180 • Mystic, CT 06355
1-800-321-0411
E-Mail:ttpubs@aol.com